Booked & Busy

READING JOURNAL

BOOKED AND BUSY READING JOURNAL

© Copyright 2025 Publish Her Press

ISBN: 978-1-962457-52-1 (Softcover)

Printed in the United States of America

Published by Publish Her, LLC
6726 Walker Street
St. Louis Park, MN 55426
www.publishherpress.com

Publish Her is a female-founded publisher dedicated to
educating authors and elevating the words, stories
and writing of women.

PUBLISH **HER**™

HOW TO USE THIS JOURNAL

Track and organize the books you read and record your thoughts in this specialty journal for booklovers. It's designed to be used with or without a mini printer (not included).

The front pages of this journal serve as a book tracker. List the books you read, the authors, and the page numbers that correspond to your journal entries, so you can quickly refer to them later.

Next, you'll find guided journaling pages. They include space for cover art, which you can print and paste into your journal. Or doodle your own! Prompts help you rate characters, plot, writing and the overall book, with dedicated space for your reviews. There's also room to note highlights, quotes and questions.

This journal is designed to fit in your purse, backpack or tote bag, so you can easily jot down notes on the go. Keep it with you to share your thoughts during bookish conversations with friends or discussions with book club members.

It's a lasting keepsake to help you remember your favorite books and what you loved most about them.

BOOK TRACKER

Pages	Book Title _____
2-3	Author _____

Pages	Book Title _____
4-5	Author _____

Pages	Book Title _____
6-7	Author _____

Pages	Book Title _____
8-9	Author _____

Pages	Book Title _____
10-11	Author _____

Pages	Book Title _____
12-13	Author _____

Pages	Book Title _____
14-15	Author _____

Pages	Book Title _____
16-17	Author _____

Pages	Book Title _____
18-19	Author _____

Pages	Book Title _____
20-21	Author _____

Pages	Book Title _____
22–23	Author _____

Pages	Book Title _____
24–25	Author _____

Pages	Book Title _____
26–27	Author _____

Pages	Book Title _____
28–29	Author _____

Pages	Book Title _____
30–31	Author _____

Pages	Book Title _____
32–33	Author _____

Pages	Book Title _____
34–35	Author _____

Pages	Book Title _____
36–37	Author _____

Pages	Book Title _____
38–39	Author _____

Pages	Book Title _____
40–41	Author _____

Pages	Book Title _____
42-43	Author _____

Pages	Book Title _____
44-45	Author _____

Pages	Book Title _____
46-47	Author _____

Pages	Book Title _____
48-49	Author _____

Pages	Book Title _____
50-51	Author _____

Pages	Book Title _____
52-53	Author _____

Pages	Book Title _____
54-55	Author _____

Pages	Book Title _____
56-57	Author _____

Pages	Book Title _____
58-59	Author _____

Pages	Book Title _____
60-61	Author _____

Pages	Book Title _____
62-63	Author _____

Pages	Book Title _____
64-65	Author _____

Pages	Book Title _____
66-67	Author _____

Pages	Book Title _____
68-69	Author _____

Pages	Book Title _____
70-71	Author _____

Pages	Book Title _____
72-73	Author _____

Pages	Book Title _____
74-75	Author _____

Pages	Book Title _____
76-77	Author _____

Pages	Book Title _____
78-79	Author _____

Pages	Book Title _____
80-81	Author _____

Pages
82-83

Book Title _____

Author _____

Pages
84-85

Book Title _____

Author _____

Pages
86-87

Book Title _____

Author _____

Pages
88-89

Book Title _____

Author _____

Pages
90-91

Book Title _____

Author _____

Pages
92-93

Book Title _____

Author _____

Pages
94-95

Book Title _____

Author _____

Pages
96-97

Book Title _____

Author _____

Pages
98-99

Book Title _____

Author _____

Pages
100-101

Book Title _____

Author _____

Pages	Book Title _____
102–103	Author _____

Pages	Book Title _____
104–105	Author _____

Pages	Book Title _____
106–107	Author _____

Pages	Book Title _____
108–109	Author _____

Pages	Book Title _____
110–111	Author _____

Pages	Book Title _____
112–113	Author _____

Pages	Book Title _____
114–115	Author _____

Pages	Book Title _____
116–117	Author _____

Pages	Book Title _____
118–119	Author _____

Pages	Book Title _____
120–121	Author _____

Pages	Book Title _____
122–123	Author _____

Pages	Book Title _____
124–125	Author _____

Pages	Book Title _____
126–127	Author _____

Pages	Book Title _____
128–129	Author _____

Pages	Book Title _____
130–131	Author _____

Pages	Book Title _____
132–133	Author _____

Pages	Book Title _____
134–135	Author _____

Pages	Book Title _____
136–137	Author _____

Pages	Book Title _____
138–139	Author _____

Pages	Book Title _____
140–141	Author _____

Pages	Book Title
142–143	Author

Pages	Book Title
144–145	Author

Pages	Book Title
146–147	Author

Pages	Book Title
148–149	Author

Pages	Book Title
150–151	Author

Pages	Book Title
152–153	Author

Pages	Book Title
154–155	Author

Pages	Book Title
156–157	Author

Pages	Book Title
158–159	Author

Pages	Book Title
160–161	Author

Pages	Book Title _____
162–163	Author _____

Pages	Book Title _____
164–165	Author _____

Pages	Book Title _____
166–167	Author _____

Pages	Book Title _____
168–169	Author _____

Pages	Book Title _____
170–171	Author _____

Pages	Book Title _____
172–173	Author _____

Pages	Book Title _____
174–175	Author _____

Pages	Book Title _____
176–177	Author _____

Pages	Book Title _____
178–179	Author _____

Pages	Book Title _____
180–181	Author _____

Pages	Book Title
182–183	Author

Pages	Book Title
184–185	Author

Pages	Book Title
186–187	Author

Pages	Book Title
188–189	Author

Pages	Book Title
190–191	Author

Pages	Book Title
192–193	Author

Pages	Book Title
194–195	Author

Pages	Book Title
196–197	Author

Pages	Book Title
198–199	Author

Pages	Book Title
200–201	Author

READING JOURNAL

Book Title and Author or Cover Art	Genre _____
	Format _____
	Number of Pages _____
	Date Started _____
	Date Finished _____
	Recommend _____
	_____
	_____

Characters	Plot	Writing	Overall
☆☆☆☆☆	☆☆☆☆☆	☆☆☆☆☆	☆☆☆☆☆

Review _____

_____

_____

_____

_____

_____

_____

_____

_____

_____

_____

_____

Highlights and Quotes _____

_____

_____

_____

_____

_____

_____

Questions _____

_____

_____

_____

_____

_____

Playlist _____

_____

_____

_____

_____

_____

Book Title and Author or Cover Art	Genre _____
	Format _____
	Number of Pages _____
	Date Started _____
	Date Finished _____
	Recommend _____
	_____
	_____

Characters	Plot	Writing	Overall
☆☆☆☆☆	☆☆☆☆☆	☆☆☆☆☆	☆☆☆☆☆

Review _____

_____

_____

_____

_____

_____

_____

_____

_____

_____

_____

_____

_____

Highlights and Quotes _____

_____

_____

_____

_____

_____

_____

_____

Questions _____

_____

_____

_____

_____

_____

_____

_____

Playlist _____

_____

_____

_____

_____

_____

_____

_____

Book Title and Author or Cover Art	Genre _____
	Format _____
	Number of Pages _____
	Date Started _____
	Date Finished _____
	Recommend _____
	_____
	_____

Characters	Plot	Writing	Overall
☆☆☆☆☆	☆☆☆☆☆	☆☆☆☆☆	☆☆☆☆☆

Review _____

_____

_____

_____

_____

_____

_____

_____

_____

_____

_____

_____

_____

Highlights and Quotes _____

_____

_____

_____

_____

_____

_____

Questions _____

_____

_____

_____

_____

_____

Playlist _____

_____

_____

_____

_____

_____

Book Title and Author or Cover Art	Genre _____
	Format _____
	Number of Pages _____
	Date Started _____
	Date Finished _____
	Recommend _____
	_____
	_____

Characters   Plot   Writing   Overall
☆☆☆☆☆   ☆☆☆☆☆   ☆☆☆☆☆   ☆☆☆☆☆

Review _____

_____

_____

_____

_____

_____

_____

_____

_____

_____

_____

_____

Highlights and Quotes _____

_____

_____

_____

_____

_____

_____

Questions _____

_____

_____

_____

_____

_____

Playlist _____

_____

_____

_____

_____

_____

Book Title and Author or Cover Art	Genre _____
	Format _____
	Number of Pages _____
	Date Started _____
	Date Finished _____
	Recommend _____
	_____
	_____

Characters	Plot	Writing	Overall
☆☆☆☆☆	☆☆☆☆☆	☆☆☆☆☆	☆☆☆☆☆

Review _____

_____

_____

_____

_____

_____

_____

_____

_____

_____

_____

_____

_____

_____

Highlights and Quotes _____

_____

_____

_____

_____

_____

_____

Questions _____

_____

_____

_____

_____

_____

Playlist _____

_____

_____

_____

_____

_____

Book Title and Author or Cover Art	Genre _____
	Format _____
	Number of Pages _____
	Date Started _____
	Date Finished _____
	Recommend _____
	_____
	_____

Characters	Plot	Writing	Overall
☆☆☆☆☆	☆☆☆☆☆	☆☆☆☆☆	☆☆☆☆☆

Review _____

_____

_____

_____

_____

_____

_____

_____

_____

_____

_____

Highlights and Quotes _____

_____

_____

_____

_____

_____

_____

_____

Questions _____

_____

_____

_____

_____

_____

_____

Playlist _____

_____

_____

_____

_____

_____

_____

Book Title and Author or Cover Art	Genre _____
	Format _____
	Number of Pages _____
	Date Started _____
	Date Finished _____
	Recommend _____
	_____
	_____

Characters   Plot   Writing   Overall
☆☆☆☆☆   ☆☆☆☆☆   ☆☆☆☆☆   ☆☆☆☆☆

Review _____

_____

_____

_____

_____

_____

_____

_____

_____

_____

_____

_____

Highlights and Quotes _____

_____

_____

_____

_____

_____

_____

Questions _____

_____

_____

_____

_____

_____

Playlist _____

_____

_____

_____

_____

_____

Book Title and Author or Cover Art	Genre _____
	Format _____
	Number of Pages _____
	Date Started _____
	Date Finished _____
	Recommend _____
	_____
	_____

| Characters | Plot | Writing | Overall |
| ☆☆☆☆☆ | ☆☆☆☆☆ | ☆☆☆☆☆ | ☆☆☆☆☆ |

Review _____

_____

_____

_____

_____

_____

_____

_____

_____

_____

_____

_____

Highlights and Quotes _____

_____

_____

_____

_____

_____

_____

Questions _____

_____

_____

_____

_____

_____

Playlist _____

_____

_____

_____

_____

_____

Book Title and Author or Cover Art	Genre _____
	Format _____
	Number of Pages _____
	Date Started _____
	Date Finished _____
	Recommend _____
	_____
	_____

Characters	Plot	Writing	Overall
☆☆☆☆☆	☆☆☆☆☆	☆☆☆☆☆	☆☆☆☆☆

Review _____

_____

_____

_____

_____

_____

_____

_____

_____

_____

_____

_____

Highlights and Quotes _____

_____

_____

_____

_____

_____

_____

Questions _____

_____

_____

_____

_____

_____

Playlist _____

_____

_____

_____

_____

_____

Book Title and Author or Cover Art	Genre _____

Format _____

Number of Pages _____

Date Started _____

Date Finished _____

Recommend _____

_____

_____

Characters	Plot	Writing	Overall
☆☆☆☆☆	☆☆☆☆☆	☆☆☆☆☆	☆☆☆☆☆

Review _____

_____

_____

_____

_____

_____

_____

_____

_____

_____

_____

_____

Highlights and Quotes _____

_____

_____

_____

_____

_____

_____

Questions _____

_____

_____

_____

_____

_____

Playlist _____

_____

_____

_____

_____

_____

Book Title and Author or Cover Art	Genre _____
	Format _____
	Number of Pages _____
	Date Started _____
	Date Finished _____
	Recommend _____
	_____
	_____

Characters	Plot	Writing	Overall
☆☆☆☆☆	☆☆☆☆☆	☆☆☆☆☆	☆☆☆☆☆

Review _____

_____

_____

_____

_____

_____

_____

_____

_____

_____

_____

_____

Highlights and Quotes _____

_____

_____

_____

_____

_____

_____

Questions _____

_____

_____

_____

_____

_____

Playlist _____

_____

_____

_____

_____

_____

Book Title and Author or Cover Art	Genre _____
	Format _____
	Number of Pages _____
	Date Started _____
	Date Finished _____
	Recommend _____
	_____
	_____

Characters	Plot	Writing	Overall
☆☆☆☆☆	☆☆☆☆☆	☆☆☆☆☆	☆☆☆☆☆

Review _____

_____

_____

_____

_____

_____

_____

_____

_____

_____

_____

_____

Highlights and Quotes _____

_____

_____

_____

_____

_____

_____

_____

Questions _____

_____

_____

_____

_____

_____

Playlist _____

_____

_____

_____

_____

_____

Book Title and Author or Cover Art	Genre _____
	Format _____
	Number of Pages _____
	Date Started _____
	Date Finished _____
	Recommend _____
	_____
	_____

Characters	Plot	Writing	Overall
☆☆☆☆☆	☆☆☆☆☆	☆☆☆☆☆	☆☆☆☆☆

Review _____

_____

_____

_____

_____

_____

_____

_____

_____

_____

_____

_____

Highlights and Quotes _____

_____

_____

_____

_____

_____

_____

_____

Questions _____

_____

_____

_____

_____

_____

_____

Playlist _____

_____

_____

_____

_____

_____

Book Title and Author or Cover Art	Genre _____
	Format _____
	Number of Pages _____
	Date Started _____
	Date Finished _____
	Recommend _____
	_____
	_____

Characters	Plot	Writing	Overall
☆☆☆☆☆	☆☆☆☆☆	☆☆☆☆☆	☆☆☆☆☆

Review _____

_____

_____

_____

_____

_____

_____

_____

_____

_____

_____

_____

Highlights and Quotes _____

_____

_____

_____

_____

_____

_____

Questions _____

_____

_____

_____

_____

_____

Playlist _____

_____

_____

_____

_____

_____

Book Title and Author or Cover Art	Genre _____
	Format _____
	Number of Pages _____
	Date Started _____
	Date Finished _____
	Recommend _____
	_____
	_____

Characters   Plot   Writing   Overall

☆☆☆☆☆   ☆☆☆☆☆   ☆☆☆☆☆   ☆☆☆☆☆

Review _____

_____

_____

_____

_____

_____

_____

_____

_____

_____

_____

_____

Highlights and Quotes _____

_____

_____

_____

_____

_____

_____

_____

Questions _____

_____

_____

_____

_____

_____

Playlist _____

_____

_____

_____

_____

_____

Book Title and Author or Cover Art	Genre _____
	Format _____
	Number of Pages _____
	Date Started _____
	Date Finished _____
	Recommend _____
	_____
	_____

Characters	Plot	Writing	Overall
☆☆☆☆☆	☆☆☆☆☆	☆☆☆☆☆	☆☆☆☆☆

Review _____

_____

_____

_____

_____

_____

_____

_____

_____

_____

_____

_____

_____

Highlights and Quotes _____

_____

_____

_____

_____

_____

_____

Questions _____

_____

_____

_____

_____

_____

Playlist _____

_____

_____

_____

_____

_____

33

Book Title and Author or Cover Art	Genre _____
	Format _____
	Number of Pages _____
	Date Started _____
	Date Finished _____
	Recommend _____
	_____
	_____

Characters	Plot	Writing	Overall
☆☆☆☆☆	☆☆☆☆☆	☆☆☆☆☆	☆☆☆☆☆

Review _____

_____

_____

_____

_____

_____

_____

_____

_____

_____

_____

Highlights and Quotes _____

_____

_____

_____

_____

_____

_____

Questions _____

_____

_____

_____

_____

_____

Playlist _____

_____

_____

_____

_____

_____

```
┌─────────────────────────┐
│ Book Title and Author   │
│ or Cover Art            │
│                         │
│                         │
│                         │
│                         │
│                         │
│                         │
│                         │
│                         │
│                         │
└─────────────────────────┘
```

Genre _____

Format _____

Number of Pages _____

Date Started _____

Date Finished _____

Recommend _____

_____

_____

Characters	Plot	Writing	Overall
☆☆☆☆☆	☆☆☆☆☆	☆☆☆☆☆	☆☆☆☆☆

Review _____

_____

_____

_____

_____

_____

_____

_____

_____

_____

_____

Highlights and Quotes _____

_____

_____

_____

_____

_____

_____

Questions _____

_____

_____

_____

_____

_____

Playlist _____

_____

_____

_____

_____

_____

Book Title and Author or Cover Art	Genre _____
	Format _____
	Number of Pages _____
	Date Started _____
	Date Finished _____
	Recommend _____
	_____
	_____

Characters	Plot	Writing	Overall
☆☆☆☆☆	☆☆☆☆☆	☆☆☆☆☆	☆☆☆☆☆

Review _____

_____

_____

_____

_____

_____

_____

_____

_____

_____

_____

_____

Highlights and Quotes _____

_____

_____

_____

_____

_____

_____

Questions _____

_____

_____

_____

_____

_____

Playlist _____

_____

_____

_____

_____

_____

Book Title and Author or Cover Art	Genre _____
	Format _____
	Number of Pages _____
	Date Started _____
	Date Finished _____
	Recommend _____
	_____
	_____

Characters	Plot	Writing	Overall
☆☆☆☆☆	☆☆☆☆☆	☆☆☆☆☆	☆☆☆☆☆

Review _____

_____

_____

_____

_____

_____

_____

_____

_____

_____

_____

_____

_____

Highlights and Quotes _____

_____

_____

_____

_____

_____

_____

Questions _____

_____

_____

_____

_____

_____

Playlist _____

_____

_____

_____

_____

_____

Book Title and Author or Cover Art	
	Genre _____
	Format _____
	Number of Pages _____
	Date Started _____
	Date Finished _____
	Recommend _____
	_____
	_____

Characters	Plot	Writing	Overall
☆☆☆☆☆	☆☆☆☆☆	☆☆☆☆☆	☆☆☆☆☆

Review _____

_____

_____

_____

_____

_____

_____

_____

_____

_____

_____

_____

Highlights and Quotes _____

_____

_____

_____

_____

_____

_____

Questions _____

_____

_____

_____

_____

_____

Playlist _____

_____

_____

_____

_____

_____

Book Title and Author or Cover Art

Genre _____

Format _____

Number of Pages _____

Date Started _____

Date Finished _____

Recommend _____

_____

_____

Characters   Plot   Writing   Overall
☆☆☆☆☆   ☆☆☆☆☆   ☆☆☆☆☆   ☆☆☆☆☆

Review _____

_____

_____

_____

_____

_____

_____

_____

_____

_____

_____

_____

Highlights and Quotes _____

_____

_____

_____

_____

_____

_____

_____

Questions _____

_____

_____

_____

_____

_____

Playlist _____

_____

_____

_____

_____

_____

Book Title and Author or Cover Art	Genre _____
	Format _____
	Number of Pages _____
	Date Started _____
	Date Finished _____
	Recommend _____
	_____
	_____

Characters	Plot	Writing	Overall
☆☆☆☆☆	☆☆☆☆☆	☆☆☆☆☆	☆☆☆☆☆

Review _____

_____

_____

_____

_____

_____

_____

_____

_____

_____

_____

_____

Highlights and Quotes _____

_____

_____

_____

_____

_____

_____

_____

Questions _____

_____

_____

_____

_____

_____

Playlist _____

_____

_____

_____

_____

_____

Book Title and Author or Cover Art	Genre _____
	Format _____
	Number of Pages _____
	Date Started _____
	Date Finished _____
	Recommend _____
	_____
	_____

Characters	Plot	Writing	Overall
☆☆☆☆☆	☆☆☆☆☆	☆☆☆☆☆	☆☆☆☆☆

Review _____

_____

_____

_____

_____

_____

_____

_____

_____

_____

_____

Highlights and Quotes _____

_____

_____

_____

_____

_____

_____

Questions _____

_____

_____

_____

_____

_____

Playlist _____

_____

_____

_____

_____

_____

Book Title and Author or Cover Art	Genre _____
	Format _____
	Number of Pages _____
	Date Started _____
	Date Finished _____
	Recommend _____
	_____
	_____

Characters	Plot	Writing	Overall
☆☆☆☆☆	☆☆☆☆☆	☆☆☆☆☆	☆☆☆☆☆

Review _____

_____

_____

_____

_____

_____

_____

_____

_____

_____

_____

_____

_____

Highlights and Quotes _____

_____

_____

_____

_____

_____

_____

Questions _____

_____

_____

_____

_____

_____

Playlist _____

_____

_____

_____

_____

_____

Book Title and Author or Cover Art	Genre _____
	Format _____
	Number of Pages _____
	Date Started _____
	Date Finished _____
	Recommend _____
	_____
	_____

Characters	Plot	Writing	Overall
☆☆☆☆☆	☆☆☆☆☆	☆☆☆☆☆	☆☆☆☆☆

Review _____

_____

_____

_____

_____

_____

_____

_____

_____

_____

_____

_____

_____

Highlights and Quotes _____

_____

_____

_____

_____

_____

_____

Questions _____

_____

_____

_____

_____

_____

Playlist _____

_____

_____

_____

_____

_____

Book Title and Author or Cover Art	
	Genre _____
	Format _____
	Number of Pages _____
	Date Started _____
	Date Finished _____
	Recommend _____
	_____
	_____

Characters	Plot	Writing	Overall
☆☆☆☆☆	☆☆☆☆☆	☆☆☆☆☆	☆☆☆☆☆

Review _____

_____

_____

_____

_____

_____

_____

_____

_____

_____

_____

_____

Highlights and Quotes _____

_____

_____

_____

_____

_____

_____

Questions _____

_____

_____

_____

_____

_____

Playlist _____

_____

_____

_____

_____

_____

Book Title and Author or Cover Art	

Genre _____

Format _____

Number of Pages _____

Date Started _____

Date Finished _____

Recommend _____

_____

_____

Characters	Plot	Writing	Overall
☆☆☆☆☆	☆☆☆☆☆	☆☆☆☆☆	☆☆☆☆☆

Review _____

_____

_____

_____

_____

_____

_____

_____

_____

_____

_____

_____

Highlights and Quotes _____

_____

_____

_____

_____

_____

_____

Questions _____

_____

_____

_____

_____

Playlist _____

_____

_____

_____

_____

_____

Book Title and Author or Cover Art	Genre _____
	Format _____
	Number of Pages _____
	Date Started _____
	Date Finished _____
	Recommend _____
	_____
	_____

Characters	Plot	Writing	Overall
☆☆☆☆☆	☆☆☆☆☆	☆☆☆☆☆	☆☆☆☆☆

Review _____

_____

_____

_____

_____

_____

_____

_____

_____

_____

_____

_____

_____

Highlights and Quotes _____

_____

_____

_____

_____

_____

_____

_____

Questions _____

_____

_____

_____

_____

_____

_____

Playlist _____

_____

_____

_____

_____

_____

Book Title and Author or Cover Art	Genre _____
	Format _____
	Number of Pages _____
	Date Started _____
	Date Finished _____
	Recommend _____
	_____
	_____

Characters	Plot	Writing	Overall
☆☆☆☆☆	☆☆☆☆☆	☆☆☆☆☆	☆☆☆☆☆

Review _____

_____

_____

_____

_____

_____

_____

_____

_____

_____

_____

_____

Highlights and Quotes _____

_____

_____

_____

_____

_____

_____

Questions _____

_____

_____

_____

_____

_____

Playlist _____

_____

_____

_____

_____

_____

Book Title and Author or Cover Art	Genre _____
	Format _____
	Number of Pages _____
	Date Started _____
	Date Finished _____
	Recommend _____
	_____
	_____

Characters	Plot	Writing	Overall
☆☆☆☆☆	☆☆☆☆☆	☆☆☆☆☆	☆☆☆☆☆

Review _____

_____

_____

_____

_____

_____

_____

_____

_____

_____

_____

Highlights and Quotes _____

_____

_____

_____

_____

_____

_____

Questions _____

_____

_____

_____

_____

_____

Playlist _____

_____

_____

_____

_____

_____

Book Title and Author or Cover Art	Genre _____
	Format _____
	Number of Pages _____
	Date Started _____
	Date Finished _____
	Recommend _____
	_____
	_____

Characters	Plot	Writing	Overall
☆☆☆☆☆	☆☆☆☆☆☆	☆☆☆☆☆☆	☆☆☆☆☆

Review _____

_____

_____

_____

_____

_____

_____

_____

_____

_____

_____

_____

_____

Highlights and Quotes _____

_____

_____

_____

_____

_____

_____

Questions _____

_____

_____

_____

_____

_____

Playlist _____

_____

_____

_____

_____

_____

Book Title and Author or Cover Art	Genre _____
	Format _____
	Number of Pages _____
	Date Started _____
	Date Finished _____
	Recommend _____
	_____
	_____

Characters	Plot	Writing	Overall
☆☆☆☆☆	☆☆☆☆☆	☆☆☆☆☆	☆☆☆☆☆

Review _____

_____

_____

_____

_____

_____

_____

_____

_____

_____

_____

Highlights and Quotes _____

_____

_____

_____

_____

_____

_____

Questions _____

_____

_____

_____

_____

_____

Playlist _____

_____

_____

_____

_____

_____

Book Title and Author or Cover Art	Genre _____
	Format _____
	Number of Pages _____
	Date Started _____
	Date Finished _____
	Recommend _____
	_____
	_____

Characters   Plot   Writing   Overall
☆☆☆☆☆   ☆☆☆☆☆   ☆☆☆☆☆   ☆☆☆☆☆

Review _____

_____

_____

_____

_____

_____

_____

_____

_____

_____

_____

_____

Highlights and Quotes _____

_____

_____

_____

_____

_____

_____

_____

Questions _____

_____

_____

_____

_____

_____

Playlist _____

_____

_____

_____

_____

_____

Book Title and Author or Cover Art	Genre _____
	Format _____
	Number of Pages _____
	Date Started _____
	Date Finished _____
	Recommend _____
	_____
	_____

Characters	Plot	Writing	Overall
☆☆☆☆☆	☆☆☆☆☆	☆☆☆☆☆	☆☆☆☆☆

Review _____

_____

_____

_____

_____

_____

_____

_____

_____

_____

_____

_____

_____

Highlights and Quotes _____

_____

_____

_____

_____

_____

_____

Questions _____

_____

_____

_____

_____

_____

Playlist _____

_____

_____

_____

_____

_____

| Book Title and Author or Cover Art | Genre _____ |

Format _____

Number of Pages _____

Date Started _____

Date Finished _____

Recommend _____

_____

_____

Characters	Plot	Writing	Overall
☆☆☆☆☆	☆☆☆☆☆	☆☆☆☆☆	☆☆☆☆☆

Review _____

_____

_____

_____

_____

_____

_____

_____

_____

_____

_____

_____

_____

Highlights and Quotes _____

_____

_____

_____

_____

_____

_____

Questions _____

_____

_____

_____

_____

_____

Playlist _____

_____

_____

_____

_____

_____

Book Title and Author or Cover Art	Genre _____
	Format _____
	Number of Pages _____
	Date Started _____
	Date Finished _____
	Recommend _____
	_____
	_____

Characters	Plot	Writing	Overall
☆☆☆☆☆	☆☆☆☆☆	☆☆☆☆☆	☆☆☆☆☆

Review _____

_____

_____

_____

_____

_____

_____

_____

_____

_____

_____

_____

Highlights and Quotes _____

_____

_____

_____

_____

_____

_____

Questions _____

_____

_____

_____

_____

_____

Playlist _____

_____

_____

_____

_____

_____

Book Title and Author or Cover Art	Genre _____
	Format _____
	Number of Pages _____
	Date Started _____
	Date Finished _____
	Recommend _____
	_____
	_____

Characters	Plot	Writing	Overall
☆☆☆☆☆	☆☆☆☆☆	☆☆☆☆☆	☆☆☆☆☆

Review _____

_____

_____

_____

_____

_____

_____

_____

_____

_____

_____

_____

Highlights and Quotes _____

_____

_____

_____

_____

_____

_____

Questions _____

_____

_____

_____

_____

_____

Playlist _____

_____

_____

_____

_____

_____

Book Title and Author or Cover Art

Genre _____

Format _____

Number of Pages _____

Date Started _____

Date Finished _____

Recommend _____

_____

_____

Characters	Plot	Writing	Overall
☆☆☆☆☆	☆☆☆☆☆	☆☆☆☆☆	☆☆☆☆☆

Review _____

_____

_____

_____

_____

_____

_____

_____

_____

_____

_____

_____

_____

Highlights and Quotes _____

_____

_____

_____

_____

_____

_____

Questions _____

_____

_____

_____

_____

_____

Playlist _____

_____

_____

_____

_____

_____

Book Title and Author or Cover Art	

Genre _____

Format _____

Number of Pages _____

Date Started _____

Date Finished _____

Recommend _____

_____

_____

Characters	Plot	Writing	Overall
☆☆☆☆☆	☆☆☆☆☆	☆☆☆☆☆	☆☆☆☆☆

Review _____

_____

_____

_____

_____

_____

_____

_____

_____

_____

_____

_____

Highlights and Quotes _____

_____

_____

_____

_____

_____

_____

Questions _____

_____

_____

_____

_____

_____

Playlist _____

_____

_____

_____

_____

_____

Book Title and Author or Cover Art	Genre _____
	Format _____
	Number of Pages _____
	Date Started _____
	Date Finished _____
	Recommend _____
	_____
	_____

Characters	Plot	Writing	Overall
☆☆☆☆☆	☆☆☆☆☆	☆☆☆☆☆	☆☆☆☆☆

Review _____

_____

_____

_____

_____

_____

_____

_____

_____

_____

_____

_____

_____

Highlights and Quotes _____

_____

_____

_____

_____

_____

_____

Questions _____

_____

_____

_____

_____

_____

Playlist _____

_____

_____

_____

_____

_____

Book Title and Author or Cover Art	Genre _____
	Format _____
	Number of Pages _____
	Date Started _____
	Date Finished _____
	Recommend _____
	_____
	_____

Characters	Plot	Writing	Overall
☆☆☆☆☆	☆☆☆☆☆	☆☆☆☆☆	☆☆☆☆☆

Review _____

_____

_____

_____

_____

_____

_____

_____

_____

_____

_____

_____

_____

Highlights and Quotes _____

_____

_____

_____

_____

_____

_____

Questions _____

_____

_____

_____

_____

_____

Playlist _____

_____

_____

_____

_____

_____

Book Title and Author or Cover Art	Genre _____
	Format _____
	Number of Pages _____
	Date Started _____
	Date Finished _____
	Recommend _____
	_____
	_____

Characters	Plot	Writing	Overall
☆☆☆☆☆	☆☆☆☆☆	☆☆☆☆☆	☆☆☆☆☆

Review _____

_____

_____

_____

_____

_____

_____

_____

_____

_____

_____

_____

Highlights and Quotes _____

_____

_____

_____

_____

_____

_____

Questions _____

_____

_____

_____

_____

_____

Playlist _____

_____

_____

_____

_____

_____

Book Title and Author or Cover Art	
	Genre _____
	Format _____
	Number of Pages _____
	Date Started _____
	Date Finished _____
	Recommend _____
	_____
	_____

Characters	Plot	Writing	Overall
☆☆☆☆☆	☆☆☆☆☆	☆☆☆☆☆	☆☆☆☆☆

Review _____

_____

_____

_____

_____

_____

_____

_____

_____

_____

_____

_____

Highlights and Quotes _____

_____

_____

_____

_____

_____

_____

_____

Questions _____

_____

_____

_____

_____

_____

_____

Playlist _____

_____

_____

_____

_____

_____

Book Title and Author or Cover Art	Genre _____
	Format _____
	Number of Pages _____
	Date Started _____
	Date Finished _____
	Recommend _____
	_____
	_____

Characters	Plot	Writing	Overall
☆☆☆☆☆	☆☆☆☆☆	☆☆☆☆☆	☆☆☆☆☆

Review _____

_____

_____

_____

_____

_____

_____

_____

_____

_____

_____

_____

_____

Highlights and Quotes _____

_____

_____

_____

_____

_____

_____

Questions _____

_____

_____

_____

_____

_____

Playlist _____

_____

_____

_____

_____

_____

Book Title and Author or Cover Art	Genre _____
	Format _____
	Number of Pages _____
	Date Started _____
	Date Finished _____
	Recommend _____
	_____
	_____

Characters	Plot	Writing	Overall
☆☆☆☆☆	☆☆☆☆☆	☆☆☆☆☆	☆☆☆☆☆

Review _____

_____

_____

_____

_____

_____

_____

_____

_____

_____

_____

_____

Highlights and Quotes _____

_____

_____

_____

_____

_____

_____

Questions _____

_____

_____

_____

_____

_____

Playlist _____

_____

_____

_____

_____

_____

Book Title and Author or Cover Art	Genre _____
	Format _____
	Number of Pages _____
	Date Started _____
	Date Finished _____
	Recommend _____
	_____
	_____

Characters	Plot	Writing	Overall
☆☆☆☆☆	☆☆☆☆☆	☆☆☆☆☆	☆☆☆☆☆

Review _____

_____

_____

_____

_____

_____

_____

_____

_____

_____

_____

_____

Highlights and Quotes _____

_____

_____

_____

_____

_____

_____

Questions _____

_____

_____

_____

_____

_____

Playlist _____

_____

_____

_____

_____

_____

Book Title and Author or Cover Art

Genre _____

Format _____

Number of Pages _____

Date Started _____

Date Finished _____

Recommend _____

_____

_____

Characters	Plot	Writing	Overall
☆☆☆☆☆	☆☆☆☆☆	☆☆☆☆☆	☆☆☆☆☆

Review _____

_____

_____

_____

_____

_____

_____

_____

_____

_____

_____

_____

_____

Highlights and Quotes _____

_____

_____

_____

_____

_____

_____

Questions _____

_____

_____

_____

_____

_____

Playlist _____

_____

_____

_____

_____

_____

Book Title and Author or Cover Art	
	Genre _____
	Format _____
	Number of Pages _____
	Date Started _____
	Date Finished _____
	Recommend _____
	_____
	_____

Characters	Plot	Writing	Overall
☆☆☆☆☆	☆☆☆☆☆	☆☆☆☆☆	☆☆☆☆☆

Review _____

_____

_____

_____

_____

_____

_____

_____

_____

_____

_____

_____

Highlights and Quotes _____

_____

_____

_____

_____

_____

_____

Questions _____

_____

_____

_____

_____

_____

Playlist _____

_____

_____

_____

_____

_____

Book Title and Author or Cover Art	
	Genre _____
	Format _____
	Number of Pages _____
	Date Started _____
	Date Finished _____
	Recommend _____
	_____
	_____

Characters	Plot	Writing	Overall
☆☆☆☆☆	☆☆☆☆☆	☆☆☆☆☆	☆☆☆☆☆

Review _____

_____

_____

_____

_____

_____

_____

_____

_____

_____

_____

_____

Highlights and Quotes _____

_____

_____

_____

_____

_____

_____

Questions _____

_____

_____

_____

_____

_____

Playlist _____

_____

_____

_____

_____

_____

Book Title and Author or Cover Art	Genre _____
	Format _____
	Number of Pages _____
	Date Started _____
	Date Finished _____
	Recommend _____
	_____
	_____

Characters   Plot   Writing   Overall

☆☆☆☆☆   ☆☆☆☆☆   ☆☆☆☆☆   ☆☆☆☆☆

Review _____

_____

_____

_____

_____

_____

_____

_____

_____

_____

_____

_____

Highlights and Quotes _____

_____

_____

_____

_____

_____

_____

Questions _____

_____

_____

_____

_____

_____

Playlist _____

_____

_____

_____

_____

_____

Book Title and Author or Cover Art	
	Genre _____
	Format _____
	Number of Pages _____
	Date Started _____
	Date Finished _____
	Recommend _____
	_____
	_____

Characters	Plot	Writing	Overall
☆☆☆☆☆	☆☆☆☆☆	☆☆☆☆☆	☆☆☆☆☆

Review _____

_____

_____

_____

_____

_____

_____

_____

_____

_____

_____

_____

Highlights and Quotes _____

_____

_____

_____

_____

_____

_____

Questions _____

_____

_____

_____

_____

_____

Playlist _____

_____

_____

_____

_____

_____

Book Title and Author or Cover Art	Genre _____
	Format _____
	Number of Pages _____
	Date Started _____
	Date Finished _____
	Recommend _____
	_____
	_____

Characters	Plot	Writing	Overall
☆☆☆☆☆	☆☆☆☆☆	☆☆☆☆☆	☆☆☆☆☆

Review _____

_____

_____

_____

_____

_____

_____

_____

_____

_____

_____

_____

_____

Highlights and Quotes _____

_____

_____

_____

_____

_____

_____

_____

Questions _____

_____

_____

_____

_____

_____

Playlist _____

_____

_____

_____

_____

_____

Book Title and Author or Cover Art	Genre _____
	Format _____
	Number of Pages _____
	Date Started _____
	Date Finished _____
	Recommend _____
	_____
	_____

Characters   Plot   Writing   Overall

☆☆☆☆☆   ☆☆☆☆☆   ☆☆☆☆☆   ☆☆☆☆☆

Review _____

_____

_____

_____

_____

_____

_____

_____

_____

_____

_____

Highlights and Quotes _____

_____

_____

_____

_____

_____

_____

Questions _____

_____

_____

_____

_____

_____

Playlist _____

_____

_____

_____

_____

_____

Book Title and Author or Cover Art	Genre _____
	Format _____
	Number of Pages _____
	Date Started _____
	Date Finished _____
	Recommend _____
	_____
	_____

Characters   Plot   Writing   Overall

☆☆☆☆☆   ☆☆☆☆☆   ☆☆☆☆☆   ☆☆☆☆☆

Review _____

_____

_____

_____

_____

_____

_____

_____

_____

_____

_____

_____

_____

Highlights and Quotes _____

_____

_____

_____

_____

_____

_____

Questions _____

_____

_____

_____

_____

_____

Playlist _____

_____

_____

_____

_____

_____

Book Title and Author or Cover Art	Genre _____
	Format _____
	Number of Pages _____
	Date Started _____
	Date Finished _____
	Recommend _____
	_____
	_____

Characters	Plot	Writing	Overall
☆☆☆☆☆	☆☆☆☆☆	☆☆☆☆☆	☆☆☆☆☆

Review _____

_____

_____

_____

_____

_____

_____

_____

_____

_____

_____

_____

Highlights and Quotes _____

_____

_____

_____

_____

_____

_____

Questions _____

_____

_____

_____

_____

_____

Playlist _____

_____

_____

_____

_____

_____

Book Title and Author or Cover Art	Genre _____
	Format _____
	Number of Pages _____
	Date Started _____
	Date Finished _____
	Recommend _____
	_____
	_____

Characters	Plot	Writing	Overall
☆☆☆☆☆	☆☆☆☆☆	☆☆☆☆☆	☆☆☆☆☆

Review _____

_____

_____

_____

_____

_____

_____

_____

_____

_____

_____

_____

Highlights and Quotes _____

_____
_____
_____
_____
_____
_____

Questions _____

_____
_____
_____
_____
_____
_____

Playlist _____

_____
_____
_____
_____
_____
_____

Book Title and Author or Cover Art	

Genre _____

Format _____

Number of Pages _____

Date Started _____

Date Finished _____

Recommend _____

_____

_____

Characters	Plot	Writing	Overall
☆☆☆☆☆	☆☆☆☆☆	☆☆☆☆☆	☆☆☆☆☆

Review _____

_____

_____

_____

_____

_____

_____

_____

_____

_____

_____

Highlights and Quotes _____

_____

_____

_____

_____

_____

_____

Questions _____

_____

_____

_____

_____

_____

Playlist _____

_____

_____

_____

_____

_____

Book Title and Author or Cover Art

Genre _____

Format _____

Number of Pages _____

Date Started _____

Date Finished _____

Recommend _____

_____

_____

Characters	Plot	Writing	Overall
☆☆☆☆☆	☆☆☆☆☆	☆☆☆☆☆	☆☆☆☆☆

Review _____

_____

_____

_____

_____

_____

_____

_____

_____

_____

_____

_____

Highlights and Quotes _____

_____

_____

_____

_____

_____

_____

Questions _____

_____

_____

_____

_____

_____

Playlist _____

_____

_____

_____

_____

_____

Book Title and Author or Cover Art	Genre _____
	Format _____
	Number of Pages _____
	Date Started _____
	Date Finished _____
	Recommend _____
	_____
	_____

Characters	Plot	Writing	Overall
☆☆☆☆☆	☆☆☆☆☆	☆☆☆☆☆	☆☆☆☆☆

Review _____

_____

_____

_____

_____

_____

_____

_____

_____

_____

_____

Highlights and Quotes _____

_____

_____

_____

_____

_____

_____

Questions _____

_____

_____

_____

_____

_____

Playlist _____

_____

_____

_____

_____

_____

Book Title and Author or Cover Art	Genre _____
	Format _____
	Number of Pages _____
	Date Started _____
	Date Finished _____
	Recommend _____
	_____
	_____

Characters	Plot	Writing	Overall
☆☆☆☆☆	☆☆☆☆☆	☆☆☆☆☆	☆☆☆☆☆

Review _____

_____

_____

_____

_____

_____

_____

_____

_____

_____

_____

_____

Highlights and Quotes _____

_____

_____

_____

_____

_____

_____

Questions _____

_____

_____

_____

_____

_____

Playlist _____

_____

_____

_____

_____

_____

Book Title and Author
or Cover Art

Genre _____

Format _____

Number of Pages _____

Date Started _____

Date Finished _____

Recommend _____

_____

_____

Characters	Plot	Writing	Overall
☆☆☆☆☆	☆☆☆☆☆	☆☆☆☆☆	☆☆☆☆☆

Review _____

_____

_____

_____

_____

_____

_____

_____

_____

_____

_____

_____

Highlights and Quotes _____

_____

_____

_____

_____

_____

_____

Questions _____

_____

_____

_____

_____

_____

Playlist _____

_____

_____

_____

_____

_____

Book Title and Author or Cover Art	Genre _____
	Format _____
	Number of Pages _____
	Date Started _____
	Date Finished _____
	Recommend _____
	_____
	_____

Characters	Plot	Writing	Overall
☆☆☆☆☆	☆☆☆☆☆	☆☆☆☆☆	☆☆☆☆☆

Review _____

_____

_____

_____

_____

_____

_____

_____

_____

_____

_____

Highlights and Quotes _____

_____

_____

_____

_____

_____

_____

Questions _____

_____

_____

_____

_____

_____

_____

Playlist _____

_____

_____

_____

_____

_____

_____

Book Title and Author or Cover Art	Genre _____
	Format _____
	Number of Pages _____
	Date Started _____
	Date Finished _____
	Recommend _____
	_____
	_____

Characters   Plot   Writing   Overall

☆☆☆☆☆   ☆☆☆☆☆   ☆☆☆☆☆   ☆☆☆☆☆

Review _____

_____

_____

_____

_____

_____

_____

_____

_____

_____

_____

_____

Highlights and Quotes _____

_____

_____

_____

_____

_____

_____

Questions _____

_____

_____

_____

_____

_____

_____

Playlist _____

_____

_____

_____

_____

_____

_____

Book Title and Author or Cover Art	Genre _____
	Format _____
	Number of Pages _____
	Date Started _____
	Date Finished _____
	Recommend _____
	_____
	_____

Characters	Plot	Writing	Overall
☆☆☆☆☆	☆☆☆☆☆	☆☆☆☆☆	☆☆☆☆☆

Review _____

_____

_____

_____

_____

_____

_____

_____

_____

_____

_____

_____

_____

Highlights and Quotes _____

_____

_____

_____

_____

_____

_____

Questions _____

_____

_____

_____

_____

_____

Playlist _____

_____

_____

_____

_____

_____

Book Title and Author or Cover Art	Genre _____
	Format _____
	Number of Pages _____
	Date Started _____
	Date Finished _____
	Recommend _____
	_____
	_____

Characters	Plot	Writing	Overall
☆☆☆☆☆	☆☆☆☆☆	☆☆☆☆☆	☆☆☆☆☆

Review _____

_____

_____

_____

_____

_____

_____

_____

_____

_____

_____

Highlights and Quotes _____

_____
_____
_____
_____
_____
_____

Questions _____

_____
_____
_____
_____
_____
_____

Playlist _____

_____
_____
_____
_____
_____
_____

Book Title and Author or Cover Art	Genre _____
	Format _____
	Number of Pages _____
	Date Started _____
	Date Finished _____
	Recommend _____
	_____
	_____

Characters   Plot   Writing   Overall

☆☆☆☆☆   ☆☆☆☆☆   ☆☆☆☆☆   ☆☆☆☆☆

Review _____

_____

_____

_____

_____

_____

_____

_____

_____

_____

_____

_____

Highlights and Quotes _____

_____

_____

_____

_____

_____

_____

Questions _____

_____

_____

_____

_____

_____

Playlist _____

_____

_____

_____

_____

_____

Book Title and Author or Cover Art	Genre _____
	Format _____
	Number of Pages _____
	Date Started _____
	Date Finished _____
	Recommend _____
	_____
	_____

Characters	Plot	Writing	Overall
☆☆☆☆☆	☆☆☆☆☆	☆☆☆☆☆	☆☆☆☆☆

Review _____

_____

_____

_____

_____

_____

_____

_____

_____

_____

_____

_____

Highlights and Quotes _____

_____

_____

_____

_____

_____

_____

Questions _____

_____

_____

_____

_____

_____

Playlist _____

_____

_____

_____

_____

_____

Book Title and Author or Cover Art

Genre _____

Format _____

Number of Pages _____

Date Started _____

Date Finished _____

Recommend _____

_____

_____

Characters	Plot	Writing	Overall
☆☆☆☆☆	☆☆☆☆☆	☆☆☆☆☆	☆☆☆☆☆

Review _____

_____

_____

_____

_____

_____

_____

_____

_____

_____

_____

_____

_____

Highlights and Quotes _____

_____

_____

_____

_____

_____

_____

Questions _____

_____

_____

_____

_____

_____

Playlist _____

_____

_____

_____

_____

_____

```
┌─────────────────────────┐
│ Book Title and Author   │   Genre _____
│ or Cover Art            │
│                         │   Format _____
│                         │
│                         │   Number of Pages _____
│                         │
│                         │   Date Started _____
│                         │
│                         │   Date Finished _____
│                         │
│                         │   Recommend _____
│                         │
│                         │   _____
│                         │
│                         │   _____
└─────────────────────────┘
```

Characters	Plot	Writing	Overall
☆☆☆☆☆	☆☆☆☆☆	☆☆☆☆☆	☆☆☆☆☆

Review _____

_____

_____

_____

_____

_____

_____

_____

_____

_____

_____

_____

_____

Highlights and Quotes _____

_____

_____

_____

_____

_____

_____

Questions _____

_____

_____

_____

_____

_____

Playlist _____

_____

_____

_____

_____

_____

Book Title and Author or Cover Art	Genre _____
	Format _____
	Number of Pages _____
	Date Started _____
	Date Finished _____
	Recommend _____
	_____
	_____

Characters	Plot	Writing	Overall
☆☆☆☆☆	☆☆☆☆☆	☆☆☆☆☆	☆☆☆☆☆

Review _____

_____

_____

_____

_____

_____

_____

_____

_____

_____

_____

_____

_____

Highlights and Quotes _____

_____

_____

_____

_____

_____

_____

Questions _____

_____

_____

_____

_____

_____

Playlist _____

_____

_____

_____

_____

_____

Book Title and Author or Cover Art	Genre _____
	Format _____
	Number of Pages _____
	Date Started _____
	Date Finished _____
	Recommend _____
	_____
	_____

Characters	Plot	Writing	Overall
☆☆☆☆☆	☆☆☆☆☆	☆☆☆☆☆	☆☆☆☆☆

Review _____

_____

_____

_____

_____

_____

_____

_____

_____

_____

_____

_____

Highlights and Quotes _____

_____

_____

_____

_____

_____

_____

Questions _____

_____

_____

_____

_____

_____

Playlist _____

_____

_____

_____

_____

_____

Book Title and Author
or Cover Art

Genre _____

Format _____

Number of Pages _____

Date Started _____

Date Finished _____

Recommend _____

_____

_____

Characters	Plot	Writing	Overall
☆☆☆☆☆	☆☆☆☆☆	☆☆☆☆☆	☆☆☆☆☆

Review _____

_____

_____

_____

_____

_____

_____

_____

_____

_____

_____

Highlights and Quotes _____

_____

_____

_____

_____

_____

_____

_____

Questions _____

_____

_____

_____

_____

_____

_____

Playlist _____

_____

_____

_____

_____

_____

Book Title and Author
or Cover Art

Genre _____

Format _____

Number of Pages _____

Date Started _____

Date Finished _____

Recommend _____

_____

_____

Characters	Plot	Writing	Overall
☆☆☆☆☆	☆☆☆☆☆	☆☆☆☆☆	☆☆☆☆☆

Review _____

_____

_____

_____

_____

_____

_____

_____

_____

_____

_____

Highlights and Quotes _____

_____

_____

_____

_____

_____

_____

_____

Questions _____

_____

_____

_____

_____

_____

_____

Playlist _____

_____

_____

_____

_____

_____

Book Title and Author
or Cover Art

Genre _____

Format _____

Number of Pages _____

Date Started _____

Date Finished _____

Recommend _____

_____

_____

Characters	Plot	Writing	Overall
☆☆☆☆☆	☆☆☆☆☆	☆☆☆☆☆	☆☆☆☆☆

Review _____

_____

_____

_____

_____

_____

_____

_____

_____

_____

_____

_____

_____

Highlights and Quotes _____

_____

_____

_____

_____

_____

_____

Questions _____

_____

_____

_____

_____

_____

Playlist _____

_____

_____

_____

_____

_____

Book Title and Author or Cover Art	Genre _____
	Format _____
	Number of Pages _____
	Date Started _____
	Date Finished _____
	Recommend _____
	_____
	_____

Characters	Plot	Writing	Overall
☆☆☆☆☆	☆☆☆☆☆	☆☆☆☆☆	☆☆☆☆☆

Review _____

_____

_____

_____

_____

_____

_____

_____

_____

_____

_____

_____

Highlights and Quotes _____

_____

_____

_____

_____

_____

_____

Questions _____

_____

_____

_____

_____

_____

Playlist _____

_____

_____

_____

_____

_____

Book Title and Author or Cover Art	Genre _____
	Format _____
	Number of Pages _____
	Date Started _____
	Date Finished _____
	Recommend _____
	_____
	_____

Characters	Plot	Writing	Overall
☆☆☆☆☆	☆☆☆☆☆	☆☆☆☆☆	☆☆☆☆☆

Review _____

_____

_____

_____

_____

_____

_____

_____

_____

_____

_____

_____

Highlights and Quotes _____

_____

_____

_____

_____

_____

_____

Questions _____

_____

_____

_____

_____

_____

Playlist _____

_____

_____

_____

_____

_____

```
┌─────────────────────────┐
│ Book Title and Author   │   Genre _____
│ or Cover Art            │
│                         │   Format _____
│                         │
│                         │   Number of Pages _____
│                         │
│                         │   Date Started _____
│                         │
│                         │   Date Finished _____
│                         │
│                         │   Recommend _____
│                         │
│                         │   _____
│                         │
│                         │   _____
└─────────────────────────┘
```

Characters	Plot	Writing	Overall
☆☆☆☆☆	☆☆☆☆☆	☆☆☆☆☆	☆☆☆☆☆

Review _____

_____

_____

_____

_____

_____

_____

_____

_____

_____

_____

_____

_____

Highlights and Quotes _____

_____

_____

_____

_____

_____

_____

Questions _____

_____

_____

_____

_____

_____

Playlist _____

_____

_____

_____

_____

_____

Book Title and Author or Cover Art	Genre _____
	Format _____
	Number of Pages _____
	Date Started _____
	Date Finished _____
	Recommend _____
	_____
	_____

Characters	Plot	Writing	Overall
☆☆☆☆☆	☆☆☆☆☆	☆☆☆☆☆	☆☆☆☆☆

Review _____

_____

_____

_____

_____

_____

_____

_____

_____

_____

_____

_____

Highlights and Quotes _____

_____

_____

_____

_____

_____

_____

Questions _____

_____

_____

_____

_____

_____

Playlist _____

_____

_____

_____

_____

_____

Book Title and Author or Cover Art	Genre _____
	Format _____
	Number of Pages _____
	Date Started _____
	Date Finished _____
	Recommend _____
	_____
	_____

Characters	Plot	Writing	Overall
☆☆☆☆☆	☆☆☆☆☆	☆☆☆☆☆	☆☆☆☆☆

Review _____

_____

_____

_____

_____

_____

_____

_____

_____

_____

_____

_____

Highlights and Quotes _____

_____

_____

_____

_____

_____

_____

_____

Questions _____

_____

_____

_____

_____

_____

_____

Playlist _____

_____

_____

_____

_____

_____

_____

Book Title and Author or Cover Art	Genre _____
	Format _____
	Number of Pages _____
	Date Started _____
	Date Finished _____
	Recommend _____
	_____
	_____

Characters	Plot	Writing	Overall
☆☆☆☆☆	☆☆☆☆☆	☆☆☆☆☆	☆☆☆☆☆

Review _____

_____

_____

_____

_____

_____

_____

_____

_____

_____

_____

_____

Highlights and Quotes _____

_____

_____

_____

_____

_____

_____

Questions _____

_____

_____

_____

_____

_____

Playlist _____

_____

_____

_____

_____

_____

Book Title and Author or Cover Art	Genre _____
	Format _____
	Number of Pages _____
	Date Started _____
	Date Finished _____
	Recommend _____
	_____
	_____

Characters   Plot   Writing   Overall
☆☆☆☆☆   ☆☆☆☆☆   ☆☆☆☆☆   ☆☆☆☆☆

Review _____

_____

_____

_____

_____

_____

_____

_____

_____

_____

_____

_____

Highlights and Quotes _____

_____

_____

_____

_____

_____

_____

Questions _____

_____

_____

_____

_____

_____

Playlist _____

_____

_____

_____

_____

_____

Book Title and Author or Cover Art	Genre _____
	Format _____
	Number of Pages _____
	Date Started _____
	Date Finished _____
	Recommend _____
	_____
	_____

Characters	Plot	Writing	Overall
☆☆☆☆☆	☆☆☆☆☆	☆☆☆☆☆	☆☆☆☆☆

Review _____

_____

_____

_____

_____

_____

_____

_____

_____

_____

_____

_____

Highlights and Quotes _____

_____

_____

_____

_____

_____

_____

Questions _____

_____

_____

_____

_____

_____

Playlist _____

_____

_____

_____

_____

_____

Book Title and Author or Cover Art	Genre _____
	Format _____
	Number of Pages _____
	Date Started _____
	Date Finished _____
	Recommend _____
	_____
	_____

Characters	Plot	Writing	Overall
☆☆☆☆☆	☆☆☆☆☆	☆☆☆☆☆	☆☆☆☆☆

Review _____

_____

_____

_____

_____

_____

_____

_____

_____

_____

_____

_____

Highlights and Quotes _____

_____

_____

_____

_____

_____

_____

Questions _____

_____

_____

_____

_____

_____

Playlist _____

_____

_____

_____

_____

_____

```
┌─────────────────────────┐
│ Book Title and Author   │
│ or Cover Art            │
│                         │
│                         │
│                         │
│                         │
│                         │
│                         │
│                         │
│                         │
└─────────────────────────┘
```

Genre _____

Format _____

Number of Pages _____

Date Started _____

Date Finished _____

Recommend _____

_____

_____

Characters	Plot	Writing	Overall
☆☆☆☆☆	☆☆☆☆☆	☆☆☆☆☆	☆☆☆☆☆

Review _____

_____

_____

_____

_____

_____

_____

_____

_____

_____

_____

Highlights and Quotes _____

_____

_____

_____

_____

_____

_____

Questions _____

_____

_____

_____

_____

_____

Playlist _____

_____

_____

_____

_____

_____

Book Title and Author or Cover Art	Genre _____
	Format _____
	Number of Pages _____
	Date Started _____
	Date Finished _____
	Recommend _____
	_____
	_____

Characters   Plot   Writing   Overall
☆☆☆☆☆   ☆☆☆☆☆   ☆☆☆☆☆   ☆☆☆☆☆

Review _____

_____

_____

_____

_____

_____

_____

_____

_____

_____

_____

_____

Highlights and Quotes _____

_____

_____

_____

_____

_____

_____

Questions _____

_____

_____

_____

_____

_____

Playlist _____

_____

_____

_____

_____

_____

Book Title and Author or Cover Art	Genre _____
	Format _____
	Number of Pages _____
	Date Started _____
	Date Finished _____
	Recommend _____
	_____
	_____

Characters	Plot	Writing	Overall
☆☆☆☆☆	☆☆☆☆☆	☆☆☆☆☆	☆☆☆☆☆

Review _____

_____

_____

_____

_____

_____

_____

_____

_____

_____

_____

_____

Highlights and Quotes _____

_____

_____

_____

_____

_____

_____

Questions _____

_____

_____

_____

_____

_____

Playlist _____

_____

_____

_____

_____

_____

Book Title and Author or Cover Art	Genre _____
	Format _____
	Number of Pages _____
	Date Started _____
	Date Finished _____
	Recommend _____
	_____
	_____

Characters	Plot	Writing	Overall
☆☆☆☆☆	☆☆☆☆☆	☆☆☆☆☆	☆☆☆☆☆

Review _____

_____

_____

_____

_____

_____

_____

_____

_____

_____

_____

_____

Highlights and Quotes _____

_____
_____
_____
_____
_____
_____

Questions _____

_____
_____
_____
_____
_____

Playlist _____

_____
_____
_____
_____
_____

Book Title and Author or Cover Art	Genre _____
	Format _____
	Number of Pages _____
	Date Started _____
	Date Finished _____
	Recommend _____
	_____
	_____

Characters	Plot	Writing	Overall
☆☆☆☆☆	☆☆☆☆☆	☆☆☆☆☆	☆☆☆☆☆

Review _____

_____

_____

_____

_____

_____

_____

_____

_____

_____

_____

_____

Highlights and Quotes _____

_____

_____

_____

_____

_____

_____

Questions _____

_____

_____

_____

_____

_____

Playlist _____

_____

_____

_____

_____

_____

Book Title and Author or Cover Art	Genre _____
	Format _____
	Number of Pages _____
	Date Started _____
	Date Finished _____
	Recommend _____
	_____
	_____

Characters   Plot   Writing   Overall
☆☆☆☆☆   ☆☆☆☆☆   ☆☆☆☆☆   ☆☆☆☆☆

Review _____

_____

_____

_____

_____

_____

_____

_____

_____

_____

_____

Highlights and Quotes _____

_____

_____

_____

_____

_____

_____

Questions _____

_____

_____

_____

_____

_____

Playlist _____

_____

_____

_____

_____

_____

Book Title and Author or Cover Art	Genre _____
	Format _____
	Number of Pages _____
	Date Started _____
	Date Finished _____
	Recommend _____
	_____
	_____

Characters	Plot	Writing	Overall
☆☆☆☆☆	☆☆☆☆☆	☆☆☆☆☆	☆☆☆☆☆

Review _____

_____

_____

_____

_____

_____

_____

_____

_____

_____

_____

_____

Highlights and Quotes _____

_____

_____

_____

_____

_____

_____

Questions _____

_____

_____

_____

_____

_____

Playlist _____

_____

_____

_____

_____

_____

Book Title and Author or Cover Art	Genre _____
	Format _____
	Number of Pages _____
	Date Started _____
	Date Finished _____
	Recommend _____
	_____
	_____

Characters	Plot	Writing	Overall
☆☆☆☆☆	☆☆☆☆☆	☆☆☆☆☆	☆☆☆☆☆

Review _____

_____

_____

_____

_____

_____

_____

_____

_____

_____

_____

_____

Highlights and Quotes _____

_____

_____

_____

_____

_____

Questions _____

_____

_____

_____

_____

Playlist _____

_____

_____

_____

_____

Book Title and Author or Cover Art	

Genre _____

Format _____

Number of Pages _____

Date Started _____

Date Finished _____

Recommend _____

_____

_____

Characters	Plot	Writing	Overall
☆☆☆☆☆	☆☆☆☆☆	☆☆☆☆☆	☆☆☆☆☆

Review _____

_____

_____

_____

_____

_____

_____

_____

_____

_____

_____

_____

Highlights and Quotes _____

_____

_____

_____

_____

_____

_____

Questions _____

_____

_____

_____

_____

_____

Playlist _____

_____

_____

_____

_____

_____

Book Title and Author or Cover Art	Genre _____
	Format _____
	Number of Pages _____
	Date Started _____
	Date Finished _____
	Recommend _____
	_____
	_____

Characters	Plot	Writing	Overall
☆☆☆☆☆	☆☆☆☆☆	☆☆☆☆☆	☆☆☆☆☆

Review _____

_____

_____

_____

_____

_____

_____

_____

_____

_____

_____

_____

Highlights and Quotes _____

_____

_____

_____

_____

_____

_____

Questions _____

_____

_____

_____

_____

_____

Playlist _____

_____

_____

_____

_____

_____

Book Title and Author or Cover Art	Genre _____
	Format _____
	Number of Pages _____
	Date Started _____
	Date Finished _____
	Recommend _____
	_____
	_____

Characters	Plot	Writing	Overall
☆☆☆☆☆	☆☆☆☆☆	☆☆☆☆☆	☆☆☆☆☆

Review _____

_____

_____

_____

_____

_____

_____

_____

_____

_____

_____

_____

Highlights and Quotes _____

_____

_____

_____

_____

_____

_____

Questions _____

_____

_____

_____

_____

_____

Playlist _____

_____

_____

_____

_____

_____

Book Title and Author or Cover Art	Genre _____
	Format _____
	Number of Pages _____
	Date Started _____
	Date Finished _____
	Recommend _____
	_____
	_____

Characters	Plot	Writing	Overall
☆☆☆☆☆	☆☆☆☆☆	☆☆☆☆☆	☆☆☆☆☆

Review _____

_____

_____

_____

_____

_____

_____

_____

_____

_____

_____

_____

Highlights and Quotes _____

_____

_____

_____

_____

_____

_____

_____

Questions _____

_____

_____

_____

_____

_____

Playlist _____

_____

_____

_____

_____

_____

Book Title and Author or Cover Art	Genre _____
	Format _____
	Number of Pages _____
	Date Started _____
	Date Finished _____
	Recommend _____
	_____
	_____

Characters	Plot	Writing	Overall
☆☆☆☆☆	☆☆☆☆☆	☆☆☆☆☆	☆☆☆☆☆

Review _____

_____

_____

_____

_____

_____

_____

_____

_____

_____

_____

_____

Highlights and Quotes _____

_____

_____

_____

_____

_____

_____

Questions _____

_____

_____

_____

_____

_____

Playlist _____

_____

_____

_____

_____

_____

Book Title and Author or Cover Art	Genre _____
	Format _____
	Number of Pages _____
	Date Started _____
	Date Finished _____
	Recommend _____
	_____
	_____

Characters	Plot	Writing	Overall
☆☆☆☆☆	☆☆☆☆☆	☆☆☆☆☆	☆☆☆☆☆

Review _____

_____

_____

_____

_____

_____

_____

_____

_____

_____

_____

_____

Highlights and Quotes _____

_____

_____

_____

_____

_____

_____

Questions _____

_____

_____

_____

_____

_____

Playlist _____

_____

_____

_____

_____

_____

Book Title and Author or Cover Art	Genre _____
	Format _____
	Number of Pages _____
	Date Started _____
	Date Finished _____
	Recommend _____
	_____
	_____

Characters	Plot	Writing	Overall
☆☆☆☆☆	☆☆☆☆☆	☆☆☆☆☆	☆☆☆☆☆

Review _____

_____

_____

_____

_____

_____

_____

_____

_____

_____

_____

_____

Highlights and Quotes _____

_____

_____

_____

_____

_____

_____

Questions _____

_____

_____

_____

_____

_____

Playlist _____

_____

_____

_____

_____

_____

Book Title and Author or Cover Art	Genre _____
	Format _____
	Number of Pages _____
	Date Started _____
	Date Finished _____
	Recommend _____
	_____
	_____

Characters	Plot	Writing	Overall
☆☆☆☆☆	☆☆☆☆☆	☆☆☆☆☆	☆☆☆☆☆

Review _____

_____

_____

_____

_____

_____

_____

_____

_____

_____

_____

Highlights and Quotes _____

_____

_____

_____

_____

_____

_____

Questions _____

_____

_____

_____

_____

_____

Playlist _____

_____

_____

_____

_____

_____

www.ingramcontent.com/pod-product-compliance
Lightning Source LLC
Chambersburg PA
CBHW071323120626
46546CB00002B/412